Frontier America

Authors	Linda Milliken
	Anne Hennen
Illustrator	Barb Lorseyedi

EP017 ©Highsmith® Inc. 1990, 2002, 2007
W5527 State Road 106, P.O. Box 800
Fort Atkinson, WI 53538

Table of Contents

The Hands-on Heritage series has been designed to help you bring culture to life in your classroom! Look for the "For the Teacher" headings to find information to help you prepare for activities. Simply block out these sections when reproducing pages for student use.

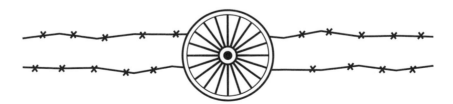

Trail Map Activities

For the Teacher
Have your students follow along with the pioneers as they travel west. Here are two choices for mapping the routes westward. Choose one or both!

Individual Trail Map
Reproduce the map on pages 4 and 5. On a larger piece of construction paper, glue or tape the pages together in the center, overlapping, to create one large map.

As students complete the trail activities that follow, they can track their progress westward. Use different colored markers or crayons for each trail.

Select other map activities appropriate to student abilities.

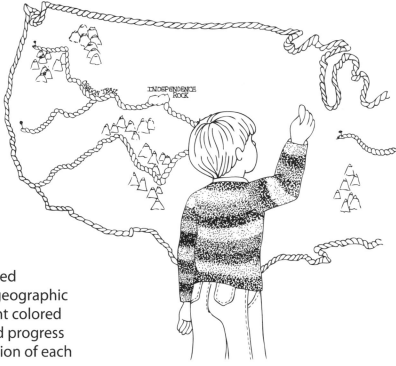

- Through what future states did the pioneers travel? What is the highest elevation of the Appalachian Mountains? The Rockies? Have students research and add geographic features to their map.

- Many pioneers, if they could write, kept journals of their daily progress. Students can write their own pioneer journals about their wagon trip west. Was it hot? What did they see? What exciting (or boring) events took place? How many miles were traveled each day?

Large-Scale Trail Map
Use yarn to recreate a huge outline of the United States on a classroom wall. Students can add geographic features using construction paper. Use different colored yarn for each trail. Keep track of your westward progress by tacking signs and pictures to note the location of each landmark. After students make their prairie schooners, tack them up along the trails. Group some in Independence, Missouri, getting ready to head out.

Get Rolling Along!
The trails were long, dusty, and tiresome; an average trip took five to six months to complete. Danger and hardships were part of daily life. But the sights were also spectacular, as you will learn as you "travel" each trail.

VANCOUVER

OREGON TRAIL

CALIFORNIA TRAIL

SACRAMENTO

OREGON TRAIL

OLD SPANISH TRAIL

SANTA FE TRAIL

OLD SPANISH TRAIL

LOS ANGELES

Santa Fe

Frontier Trail Map

EP017 Frontier America © Highsmith® Inc. 2007

CUMBERLAND

INDEPENDENCE

Westward Expansion

In the early- to mid-1800s many pioneers picked up their belongings and moved out west. There was great risks to moving a whole family out west: uncertainty, disease, lack of food, and much more, but many faced these risks for the benefits they believed moving would bring. The west was a symbol of hope for these pioneers and promised a new and better life. By moving out of the cities and farms where they were living, the pioneers hoped to be able to take more control of their own lives and better their situations.

New Land

Before 1803, the United States stretched from the east coast to the Mississippi River, and everything to the west of the Mississippi belonged to France. In 1803, President Thomas Jefferson purchased what was then known as the Louisiana Territory (which stretched from the Mississippi River to Montana, not including Texas or New Mexico) from Napoleon, the French Emporer. This Louisiana Purchase added more than 800,000 square miles (2,072,000 square km) to the United States. In 1848, the United States acquired the California, Texas, and New Mexico territories after the Mexican War.

In 1862, the Homestead Act was passed. This act gave up to 160 acres of land to any "head of household" who desired it. There was a small fee, and anyone who wanted the land needed to live on it for five years and cultivate it. Many pioneers took the government up on this offer, but few could afford to build on and work the land.

Manifest Destiny

Not all people believed that Americans should be attempting to control all of the land between the Atlantic and Pacific. However, in 1845, a man named John Louis O'Sullivan wrote an article titled "Manifest Destiny." This article supported the idea that not only was America destined to control the land, but it was America's "God-given" right.

This idea of Manifest Destiny was used to justify American movement to the west. Manifest Destiny seemed to assure pioneers that they were doing the right thing and that they would be safe and successful because God wanted them to. Manifest Destiny also justified the removal of Native Americans from the land that America wanted to acquire. However, it also inspired many pioneers to reach for a new and better life out west.

Gold and Riches

In early 1848, gold was discovered in California. News of men who had become very wealthy from the gold they discovered spread across the country. When some heard this, they rushed to California in search of their own riches. Very few of these people actually found any significant amount of gold. The more people who came in search of gold, the less any one person could find. Soon companies took over the gold mining, and most of the individuals went back to their former jobs.

EP017 Frontier America © Highsmith® Inc. 2007

Westward Expansion K-W-L Chart

Project

A K-W-L chart lists what you *Know* about a subject, what you *Want* to know about the subject, and what you *Learned* about it. Make a K-W-L chart on westward expansion.

Materials

• notebook paper

Directions

1. Before starting the unit on westward expansion, make a K-W-L chart. Fill in the chart below or create a K-W-L chart of your own on a piece of notebook paper. Make three columns: Label one K, the next W, and the last L.

2. In the K column, write what you already know about westward expansion.

3. In the W column, write what you would like to know about westward expansion. This could include any questions you have, ideas that you would like to know about, or any information you would like to get from this unit.

4. After you have finished the unit on westward expansion, list what you have learned in the L column. Were any of your questions answered? Are there still unanswered questions in your W column? If so, ask your teacher, or do your own research!

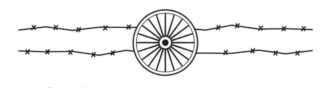

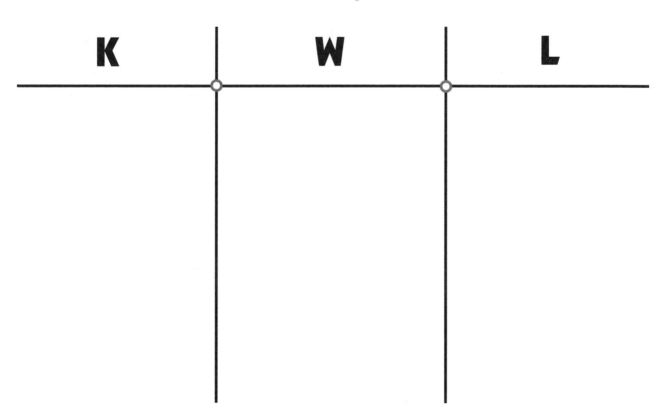

Westward Expansion

K	W	L

Early Trails

The first pioneers heading west walked or rode on horseback. They followed trails previously made by buffalo and deer or trails cut by Native Americans. Giant trees were everywhere. There were so many trees that scarcely a patch of sunlight shone through onto the forest floor.

When wagons began to roll west, these giant trees had to be cut to clear a trail. This was hard, backbreaking work. Not much distance was traveled in a day's journey.

The first trail west through the Appalachian Mountains was the Cumberland Gap. This natural pass began at the meeting point of Virginia, Kentucky, and Tennessee. Native Americans originally used the trail to follow game, such as buffalo and deer, into the lush valleys of the west. Later, its narrow, steep sides would lead the way for thousands of pioneers between 1775 and 1800.

In 1775, Daniel Boone was hired by the Transylvania Land Company to clear a trail through the pass. Blazing the road was backbreaking work. With his team of 30 woodsmen, Boone blazed a 208-mile (335-km) trail. In 1796, the trail was widened and became known as the Wilderness Road or Cumberland Road. It led from Cumberland, Maryland, to Vandalia, Illinois.

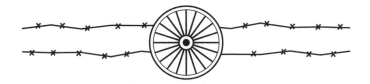

Project

Imagine all of the things along the trail that could have hindered (created difficulties for) the first pioneers.

Materials

- paper
- pencil
- white construction paper

Directions

1. On a piece of construction paper, recreate the Venn diagram below.
2. On the left, list things that helped the pioneers.
3. On the right, list things that hindered the pioneers.
4. In the middle section, list things that may have both helped and hindered the pioneers.

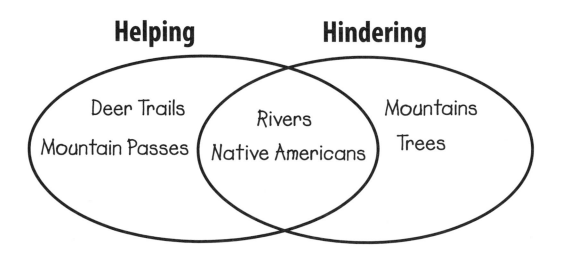

Helping   **Hindering**

Deer Trails

Mountain Passes

Rivers

Native Americans

Mountains

Trees

Transcontinental Telegraph

On October 24, 1861, Abraham Lincoln received a telegraph from Horice Carpentier that stated "I announce to you that the telegraph to California has this day been completed. May it be a bond of perpetuity between the states of the Atlantic and Pacific." This telegraph announced the completion of the first transcontinental telegraph system that stretched from St. Joseph, Missouri, to Sacramento, California.

The building of this telegraph system was difficult, especially since the Civil War made it tough to get the supplies needed. As work progressed, poles to hold the wires had to be made from trees—a task that was especially difficult in the prairie areas.

Prior to the transcontinental telegraph, the fastest way to send mail or news was through the Pony Express, which could take two weeks to deliver a message. The new telegraph system transmitted messages in minutes! This new system of communication united the nation in a way never before possible. Previously, the western states were cut off from communication with the eastern states, but the telegraph made it easy to send and receive messages quickly!

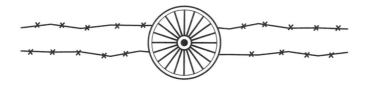

Project
Try using Morse code to send a message to a friend.

Materials
- Morse code
- notebook paper

Directions
1. Think of a message about frontier America that you would like to send to a friend.
2. Using the Morse code, encode your message. Be sure to leave spaces between each letter!
3. Trade messages with a classmate, then try to decode the message!

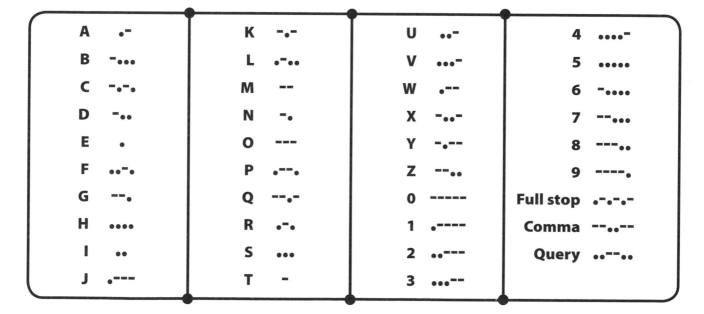

Letter	Code		Letter	Code		Letter	Code		Symbol	Code
A	.-		K	-.-		U	..-		4	....-
B	-...		L	.-..		V	...-		5	.....
C	-.-.		M	--		W	.--		6	-....
D	-..		N	-.		X	-..-		7	--...
E	.		O	---		Y	-.--		8	---..
F	..-.		P	.--.		Z	--..		9	----.
G	--.		Q	--.-		0	-----		Full stop	.-.-.-
H	....		R	.-.		1	.----		Comma	--..--
I	..		S	...		2	..---		Query	..--..
J	.---		T	-		3	...--			

Wagons Ho!

As time passed, wagons began to follow the foot and horse trails leading west. Two types of wagons were most commonly used.

The Conestoga, sometimes called the "camel of the prairie," hauled freight and people across the Alleghenies for more than 100 years. Its wheels were high so the bottom of the wagon could clear tree stumps. The end tilted up so the weight of the cargo stayed in the middle. When the wheels were removed, the wagon doubled as a boat. The Conestoga was first built by the Pennsylvania Dutch, who painted the body blue and the gear bright red. A team of six to eight horses pulled the wagon.

The Prairie Schooner was home for families and their belongings traveling to Oregon and California. It was about one-half the size of a conestoga, which was too big for oxen to pull such long distances. The wagon was called a prairie schooner because, from a distance, its white top looked like the sails of a ship. It was a standard farm wagon with very sturdy wheels. It was not built for comfort, and many travelers found it easier to walk than ride.

Shoebox Conestoga

Materials
- shoebox; white construction paper
- blue and red paint and paintbrushes
- cardboard, metal brads, pipe cleaners, or wire

Directions
1. Remove the lid and paint a shoebox blue. When the blue paint dries, paint red trim.
2. Cut four large wheels from cardboard and attach them with brads to the sides of the box.
3. Poke wire or pipe cleaners through the box at three points (see illustration). Curve the wire and fasten to the box on the opposite side.
4. Cut a piece of white material or construction paper the length of the box and wide enough to cover the wire. Glue in place.

Personalized Prairie Schooner

Materials
- Prairie Schooner Pattern
- marker and crayons

Directions
1. On the wagon's covering, write a diary entry for a day of traveling in the wagon.
2. Color and cut out the wagon.

For the Teacher
1. Copy one Prairie Schooner Pattern (page 11) for each student.
2. Post completed wagons on a bulletin board or the large-scale trail map and let students read each other's diary entries.

Prairie Schooner Pattern

Crossing Rivers

One of the first obstacles the pioneers had to overcome was crossing rivers. Sometimes, if the river was shallow and calm, the wagon could ford the river. This means that the oxen would pull the wagon across the river. For deeper rivers, the pioneers would fill spaces in their wagons with a waterproof paste and float their wagons across the river. Floating the wagon made it more likely that the wagon would tip over, but if successful, less of the contents of the wagon would get wet or lost. Deep, dangerous rivers meant that the wagon had to be put on a scow, or a large, flat boat. The scow kept the wagon from moving around much, but took longer to put together.

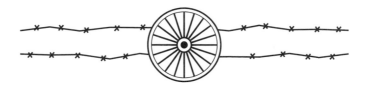

Project
Create a diorama of a pioneer family crossing a river.

Materials
- shoebox
- brown butcher paper
- craft materials: paint, construction paper, clay, etc.

Directions
1. Cover a shoebox with brown butcher paper.
2. Use paint, construction paper, clay, and other craft materials to create a shoebox diorama. Show a family, their wagon, and oxen, and illustrate how the family will get to the other side of the river.

EP017 Frontier America © Highsmith® Inc. 2007

Santa Fe and Old Spanish Trails

The Santa Fe Trail was first traveled by William Becknell in 1821 and was used for 60 years. It stretched nearly 1,000 miles (1,610 km) from Franklin, Missouri, to Santa Fe, New Mexico. The trail cut across prairies, mountains, and deserts. It had two branches. The northern branch was difficult for wagon travel. The southern branch was shorter, but had no source for water.

The Santa Fe Trail was mainly used as a commercial route. Traders took manufactured goods to Santa Fe to exchange for mules, furs, gold, and silver with the Spanish inhabitants.

Wagon Mound was a familiar landmark to passing travelers. Its shape seemed to resemble a prairie schooner. When pioneers reached Wagon Mound they knew Santa Fe was only 100 miles (160 km) beyond.

The 200-year-old Spanish colonial city of Santa Fe was a major destination for those traveling the Santa Fe Trail. Upon arriving, weary travelers were greeted by the colorful sight of ristas (strings) of chili peppers hanging in the hot sun.

The Old Spanish Trail was an extension of the Santa Fe Trail. It ran from Santa Fe, New Mexico, to Los Angeles, California, by way of Durango, Colorado, along the Colorado River and across the Mohave Desert. While not one of the more dangerous trails, the route, nevertheless, was parched and lacked an abundant water supply.

Along the way, travelers saw the buttes, mesas, peaks, and valleys that make up the desert. The setting sun was welcome relief from the heat that beat upon the wagon travelers all day.

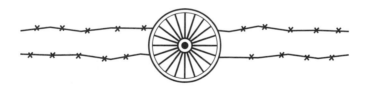

Wagon Mound

Write or draw directions to your home using only landmarks and no street names.

Materials
- paper
- pencil

Directions
1. Pretend you have to tell someone how to get from your school to your home. Write landmarks they could look for to help them get to your house. Try not to use street names.
2. If you wish, draw a map with all of the landmarks included.

Oregon and California Trails

Not many miles out of Independence, Missouri, the travelers encountered a road sign that said, "Oregon Trail." This simple sign was hardly any indication of the difficult journey that lay ahead! This was the longest of the overland routes to the west used by the pioneers, winding more than 2,000 miles (3,220 km) through prairies, deserts, and across mountains. The trail headed through what are now the states of Kansas and Nebraska, and along the Platte River. Food, water, and wood were scarce. The trail ended with a journey down the Columbia River to the Willamette Valley in Oregon.

The California Trail branched off from the Oregon Trail and headed southwest 800 miles (1200 km) through the Sierra Nevada Mountains. The route was a treacherous climb. No time could be lost as the wagon trains were in a race with the potential of an early winter's snow to get to their final destination—Sacramento, California.

The first major geographic landmark the pioneers encountered along the Oregon Trail was Chimney Rock. The spire of Chimney Rock rises about 500 feet (150 m) above the Platte River, enabling the pioneers to see it from miles away. For the pioneers, Chimney Rock signified the end of the prairie, and the beginning of the rocky, mountainous terrain.

Independence Rock, a huge block of granite, almost 650 yards (580 m) long, is on the north bank of the Sweetwater River, about 45 miles (72 km) southwest of Casper, Wyoming. It is called Independence Rock because all wagon trains tried to reach this point before the Fourth of July. That meant good progress was being made. One traveler said the rock reminded him of a "huge whale" rising above the plains. Hundreds of pioneers scratched their names on Independence Rock before continuing on their journey.

Project
Write a story about arriving at either Chimney or Independence Rock.

Materials
- notebook paper
- pen or pencil

For the Teacher
1. Create a cover for a class book of stories from the trails.
2. Bind all stories together with cover and display!

Directions
1. Imagine that you are a pioneer on either the Oregon or California trail. You have been traveling for a long time, and you can see one of these landmarks in the distance. Use vivid language to describe what you see, hear, smell, and feel. Be sure to give your characters names and personalities.
2. After you finish, create a class book of stories from the trails!

Extension Activity
Find out about the ill-fated Donner Party and the fascinating tale of their wagon journey along the California Trail and over the Sierra Nevada Mountains. Write a one-page summary of their trip and share it with the class.

EP017 Frontier America © Highsmith® Inc. 2007

You Can't Take It With You

Pioneers heading west had to know what things to take and what to leave behind. Certain equipment was necessary for the journey and building a new frontier home. The earliest pioneers took only what they could carry or load on horseback. Families traveling by wagon packed what fit into about a 5 x 10-foot space!

Most pioneers took along very basic tools, such as a hammer, saw, hoe, axe, and plow that could be used for basic building and farming. Necessary household goods such as a few pots and pans, a large iron kettle, some blankets, and perhaps a spinning wheel were also taken. Many took only the clothes they wore, but some brought cloth, needles, scissors, and leather to repair shoes. They packed sacks of cornmeal, salt pork, and dried beef. A lantern, compass, and rope were valuable possessions. A rifle and ammunition were important for daily life. Few luxuries were taken; if room permitted, a clock and a Bible were packed.

Many keepsakes, family treasures, and valuable objects were left behind. These were difficult choices for the pioneers to make but they knew that the things needed for daily life were the most important possessions of all on the frontier.

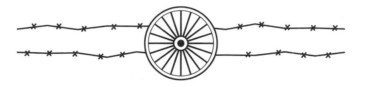

Project
Make decisions about what to take when heading west on a wagon trip.

Materials
- large piece of construction paper
- Supply Page

Directions
1. Fold your piece of construction paper in half. Label one half "TAKE" and the other half "LEAVE."
2. Color and cut out the items on the supply picture page. Decide which items to take and which to leave behind and paste them on the correct half of the paper. Number your choices in order of importance.

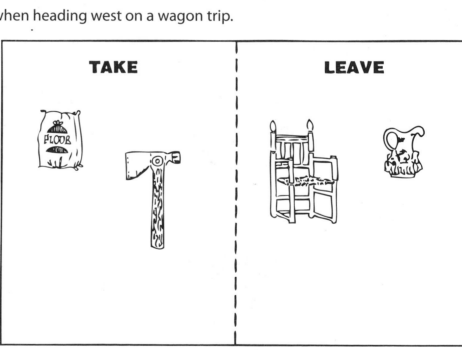

For the Teacher
Make a copy of the Supply Page (page 16) for each student. Mark off a 5 x 10-foot (1.5 x 3 m) area in the classroom so the students have an idea of the available packing space on a covered wagon. Compare and discuss their choices.

Supply Page

EP017 Frontier America © Highsmith® Inc. 2007

Scout and Wagon Master

An average of 25 wagons banded together to form a "train" heading west. Besides the elected position of a wagon master from among the male passengers, a male scout, who had usually been a fur trapper or trader, was hired to lead the way.

The wagon master was in charge. He made the final decisions, kept order on the trail, delegated responsibilities, and ensured safe travel as best he could.

A scout marked the trail for the wagon master to follow by bending sapling branches down. He also traveled ahead to find water sources, locate native people who might present problems for the pioneers, and check for any other problems on the trail. He might be gone for days, then rejoin the train and guide the way.

"Circle the wagons!" was a familiar cry heard on the trail. At the end of each day of travel, or in the event of an attack, the wagon master would lead the wagons into a large circle. This created a good windbreak and a defensive barricade.

The wagon master had to know just how large to make the circle so that the lead wagon closed the circle next to the last wagon.

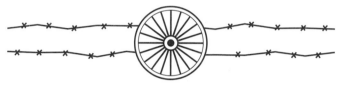

For the Teacher

Project

Play a wagon train game.

Materials

- playground, field, or permission to use the hallways
- poker chips or another type of colorful marker

Directions

1. Choose a scout to leave a trail through the school or on the playground.
2. Tell the scout where to start and end the trail. Let him or her leave colorful markers (such as poker chips) to lead the wagon train to its destination.
3. Take the class to the starting point. Tell them that they are now a wagon train and need to find their way to an unknown destination just by following the markers. (Option: to involve more students, pick more than one scout and form smaller wagon trains.)

Pioneer Men

The constant hard work, inadequate shelter, and threat of attack from animals or Native Americans required strong, capable men. With meager tools, frontier men chopped down trees on their land and built their homes out of the logs. Once the house was built, the men were in charge of working the fields so that the family could eat the crops. The man's jobs included plowing and tending to the fields, which was extremely difficult with just a wooden plow and a horse or ox. Pioneer men were also in charge of hunting and fishing. Because of the hard physical labor they did, the life expectancy of a pioneer man was 35 to 38 years.

For early pioneer men in the Appalachian regions, just getting dressed was a difficult task. Clothes were made from deerskin stitched together with sinews from the animal. Once wet, buckskin dried as stiff as a board. However, it was a good windbreaker and very protective against thorns and snakes. Just imagine your pants standing up, waiting for you to put them on!

Men on the western frontier wore the same plain garments every day. A wool shirt, vest, felt hat, blue jeans (thanks to a man named Levi Strauss), boots, and an occasional pair of socks made up his wardrobe. He often wore a red bandanna handkerchief around his neck to protect himself from dust and cold weather.

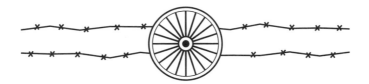

Project

Make a fringed buckskin shirt to wear.

Directions

1. Use the illustration as a guide to cut a pattern from butcher paper. Measure from just below the waist, over the shoulder, and back to the waist again to determine size.

2. Cut as shown by the dotted lines.

3. Punch holes as far as a hole punch will reach from the edge of the paper (as indicated by dots) every 2 inches (5 cm).

4. Match sides and holes; stitch with yarn or string.

5. Add fringe to the stitching.

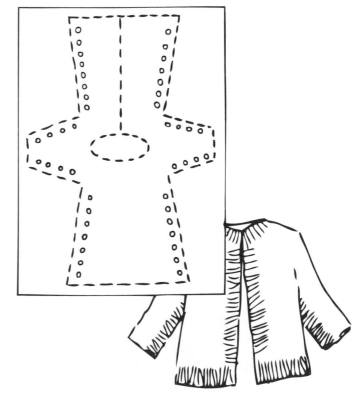

Pioneer Women

The women who helped settle the frontier shared the same risks as the men. Life expectancy for these hard-working women was 38 to 40 years. They washed, cooked, and baked with minimal supplies. They served as doctors for the ill and caretakers for the children. They spun wool and linen yarn and made all of their family's clothing. While the men worked the fields, the women cared for the chickens and cows, weeded the vegetable gardens, and taught their children.

A frontier woman wore a simple calico or gingham dress covered by an apron and a shawl for warmth. She wore a sunbonnet with a wide brim to protect her face from the harsh sun in summer.

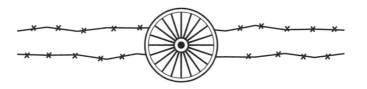

Project

Make a sunbonnet and a shawl to dress like a frontier woman.

Sunbonnet

Materials

- construction paper
- tissue paper
- ribbon

Directions

1. Fold 18 x 5-inch (46 x 13 cm) construction paper in half, lengthwise. Cut as shown by the dotted lines to make the brim.

2. Fold a 16 x 14-inch (41 cm x 35.5) piece of tissue paper in half lengthwise and cut as shown. This will be the crown.

3. Make several pleats in the curved edge of the tissue. Staple to the straight edge of the brim.

4. Pleat the bottom edge of the tissue and staple to a length of ribbon for tying under the chin.

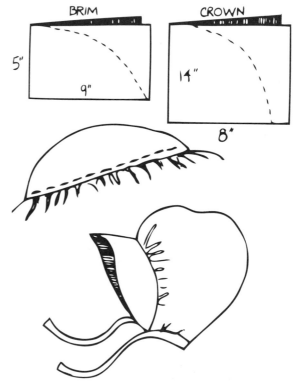

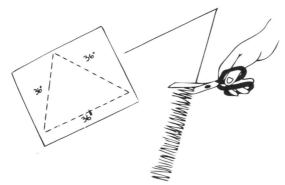

Shawl

Materials

- fabric or butcher paper

Directions

1. Cut a large triangle with three 36-inch (91-cm) sides from fabric or butcher paper.

2. Fringe two sides. Tie around the shoulders.

Life on the Trail

Traveling the trails was a long and difficult journey. A wagon could travel up to 15 miles (24 km) in one day, but only in the best weather. If it was rainy and the ground was muddy, a wagon might only travel one mile (1.6 km)! The pioneers would wake up before sunrise every morning and then travel until about an hour or two before sunset. When the wagon stopped for the night, the women would begin cooking dinner, the men would take care of the animals, and the children would gather wood for the fire.

While on the trail, there were no doctors or hospitals, so sometimes even the slightest illnesses could result in death. The Native Americans taught the pioneers to use herbs to cure sicknesses, but these herbs couldn't cure everything. Cholera and smallpox were common causes of death among travelers.

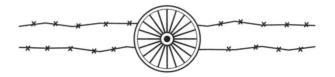

Project
Compare life on the trail to traveling today.

Materials
- notebook paper
- pencil or pen

Directions
1. Make a list of experiences that the pioneers had when they were traveling on the trail. These can be both negative and positive experiences. Do the same for travel today. What are some positive and negative experiences that travelers today experience?

2. Create a Venn diagram. Label one circle "Pioneer Trail" and the other "Today's Travel."

3. Write the pioneer experiences from your list into the "Pioneer Trail" circle, and write experiences from today in "Today's Travel."

4. Write any experiences that both groups share in the middle.

5. Discuss as a class what you found to be common experiences. What did the pioneers face that we could never dream of? What do we face that they could never dream of?

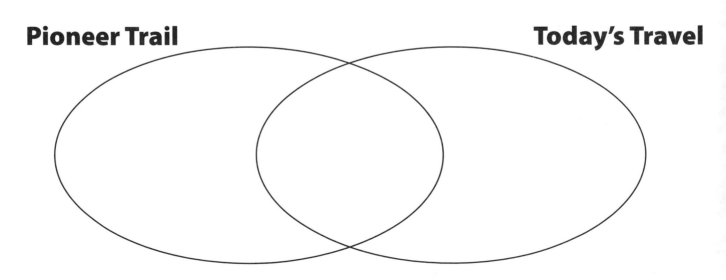

Pioneer Trail   **Today's Travel**

Barbed Wire

Wood was scarce on the prairies and plains of the western frontier. Pioneer farmers planted thick, thorny shrubs instead of building fences to contain their livestock. The invention of barbed wire in 1874 was inspired by these thorned shrubs.

The idea was simple. Two or more steel wires were twisted together to create a barbed effect. This enabled farmers to fence in their homesteads and kept free-roaming cattle off their property. Ranchers were not happy with the new invention because it brought an end to the open range. Their cattle were no longer free to graze where they liked.

However, itt was due to this simple invention that the pioneers were able to settle the frontier and prosper.

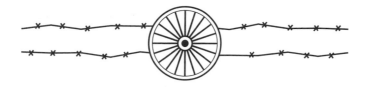

Project

Make an invention time line.

Materials

- paper
- pencil or pen
- research materials

Directions

1. Think of other inventions that changed the way people lived and worked.
2. Research these inventions. Find out the years they were invented and what they were used for.
3. Create a time line. Draw pictures of each invention and write a short description of how the inventions changed lives. Be sure to include barbed wire in 1874.

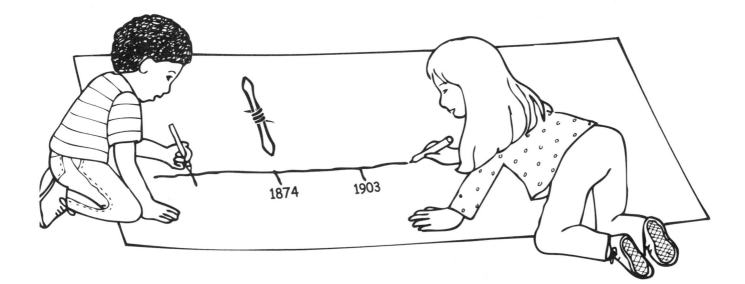

The Cactus

As the pioneers traveled west, the landscape changed greatly from what they were used to in their eastern environment.

The trail was dusty and dry. One of the strangest new plants the pioneers encountered was the cactus plant, which was found in great abundance.

There are many different types of cactus. These plants shed their leaves and make food in their stems. Most cactus plants are protected by sharp bristles and spines that protect them against animals that live in the desert. The pioneers found many uses for these unusual plants.

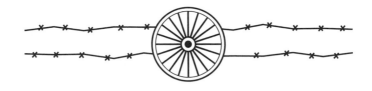

Project

Make a booklet describing the different uses for a cactus.

Materials

- research materials
- construction paper
- pen or pencil
- markers or crayons

Directions

1. Research different uses for cacti. Be sure to find out if different cacti can be used for different purposes. What did the pioneers use cacti for, and what do we use them for today?

2. Fold a few pieces of construction paper together, and staple the fold to form a booklet. Fill the pages with the information about how cacti are used.

3. Illustrate your booklet by drawing each type of cactus you researched.

For the Teacher

Project

Decorate your classroom with things that would have been new to the pioneers.

Materials

- construction paper
- markers or crayons

Directions

1. Have your class brainstorm a list of things that would have been a new sight to the pioneers.

2. Have each student create a picture of one of the new sights, and post them around the classroom.

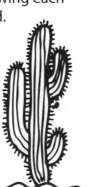

EP017 Frontier America © Highsmith® Inc. 2007

Sheriff

There were no courts or law officers in the early pioneer settlements. People needed to work together peacefully just to survive. But if problems arose, they were usually solved with fists and guns.

As towns developed on the western frontier, so did trouble with outlaws and robbers. Some towns hired a sheriff, also called a marshal, to enforce some order.

Being sheriff was dangerous and difficult. Most men carried weapons and fought freely on the streets. When someone committed a crime, a "wanted" poster appeared in frontier communities. Settlers armed themselves and rode after the outlaws themselves. An outlaw who was captured might be shot or hanged.

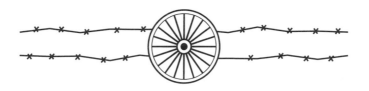

Project
Become sheriff for the day and write a wanted poster.

Materials
- Wanted poster
- Pencil

Directions
1. Research some famous outlaws from the frontier. Find out their names, what they were wanted for, where they committed their crimes, and what sort of reward was offered for their captures.
2. Use the Wanted poster to draw a picture of the outlaw and detail information about him or her.

For the Teacher
Copy one Wanted poster (page 24) per student.

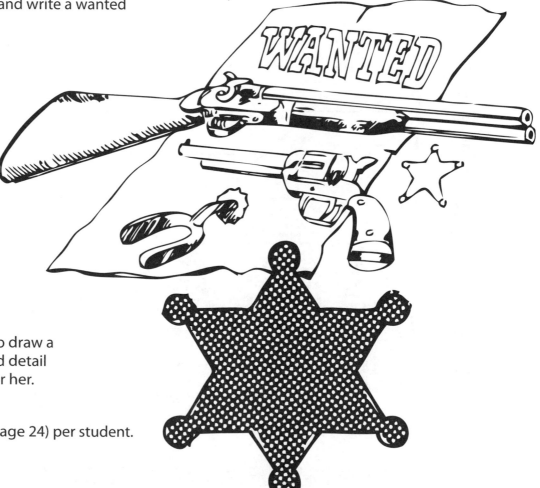

WANTED

REWARD

$

Sheriff _____

Wagon Trains West

Wagon trains with as many as 100 families gathered in and departed from Independence, Missouri, bound for the far western frontier.

They chose either the Oregon Trail, heading northwest, or the Santa Fe Trail, heading southwest.

Wagons were on the trail by early spring to avoid harsh winter weather. Before the train left Independence, officers were elected. Each wagon master's decisions along the trail became law. Wagons were grouped in two divisions, each with a captain. Both divisions were subdivided into platoons of four wagons each. A scout was hired to lead the way, select camp sites, and act as an advisor.

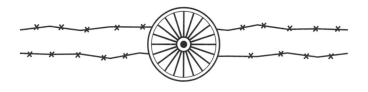

Project
Before you head your wagons west, follow the same procedures as the pioneers.

Materials
- butcher paper
- black markers

Directions
1. Elect a wagon master and officers, divide into divisions and platoons, and select a scout.

2. Work in groups of about four students to write some laws for the people on the wagon train. Remember to keep in mind some of the trouble that might arise—fighting, lack of water, Native American attacks, and weather conditions.

3. Write these laws on parchment (butcher paper) and post them for all to see. Compare and discuss the laws various groups created.

Frontier Food

As one might imagine, food on the frontier was simple. Flour was an important staple because it was nourishing, and it stored well. Flour was used in biscuits, bread, and pancakes (called flapjacks).

Dried beans, wild game animals, such as deer and bison, and preserved meats were also eaten. Rarely were the frontier families lucky enough to eat fresh fruits, vegetables, or dairy products.

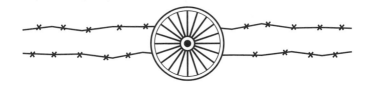

Project

Taste some food similar to frontier food.

Materials

As needed for each recipe.

Directions

Follow the directions on each recipe to get a taste of the west!

Flapjacks

2½ cups (600 ml) sifted all-purpose flour

2 Tbsp. (30 ml) baking powder

2 Tbsp. (30 ml) sugar

1 tsp. (5 ml) salt

2 beaten eggs

2 cups (480 ml) milk

4 Tbsp. (60 ml) vegetable oil

Sift together dry ingredients.
Combine eggs, milk, and oil. Add to dry mixture. Stir until flour is moistened (batter will be lumpy). Bake on hot griddle. Makes 24 silver dollar-size pancakes.

Biscuits

4 cups (960 ml) sifted all-purpose flour

2 Tbsp. (30 ml) baking powder

1 tsp. (5 ml) salt

½ cup (120 ml) shortening

2 cups (480 ml) milk

Cut shortening into sifted dry ingredients. Make a well in the center. Add milk. Stir quickly with a fork until dough follows fork around the bowl. Drop from teaspoon onto greased cookie sheet.
Bake at 450° F (232° C), 12–15 minutes. Makes 32 biscuits.

EP017 Frontier America © Highsmith® Inc. 2007

Contact with Native Americans

The western frontier was first inhabited by Native Americans. Before the pioneers began making their way west, fur trappers had already made contact trading with the Native Americans. These Native Americans were mostly friendly and interested in learning from and teaching the traders. As more pioneers began to flood into the west, there were more conflicts between the two groups. Native Americans viewed the land as a place to live on but not something that could be owned, and the pioneers believed that the Native Americans were nomads who had no desire for the land. In an attempt to protect themselves and their land, the Native Americans attacked the wagon trains from time to time.

Forts were built along the trails to serve not only as trading posts and resting spots but also as protection against attacks from Native Americans. Some famous frontier forts were Bridger, Laramie, Sutter, and McKenzie.

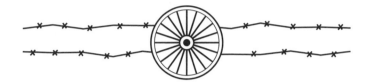

Project

Make a diorama of either a fort or a Native American settlement.

Materials

- craft sticks
- glue
- research materials

Fort

Directions

1. Research one of the forts above.
2. Using craft sticks and glue, create a model of a fort like the one found in your research.
3. Share with the class what you learned about this fort. Where was it located? How far along the trail was it? What could pioneers do there?

Native American Home

Directions

1. Research the kinds of Native American homes that pioneers may have encountered along the trail.
2. Using craft sticks and glue, create a model of a Native American home.
3. Share with the class what kind of Native American home you made. What is it called? Is there a certain tribe or region that uses this type of home? Were they permanent or temporary homes?

Railroads

As the country began expanding west, it was necessary to create newer, faster ways to get from place to place. In 1862 Congress decided to loan money to two railroad companies to build one transcontinental railroad. The Union Pacific started from Omaha, Nebraska, and headed west, and the Central Pacific started in northern California and headed east. The two railroads met at Promontory Point, Utah, on May 10, 1869.

The railroads were a very important part of the westward expansion of America. However, to build these railroads, thousands of immigrants, especially Chinese and Irish, risked their lives. The laying of tracks was dangerous work, especially because of the difficult mountainous terrain of the west.

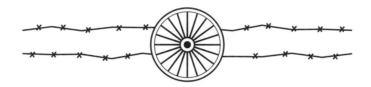

Project

Write a newspaper article about the meeting of the Union Pacific and the Central Pacific.

Materials

- notebook paper
- pencil or pen
- research materials

Directions

1. Read more about the transcontinental railroad and its final meeting at Promontory Point, Utah. Who was there? What happened? Why was it such a big deal?

2. Write a news article as if you were at Promontory Point. Make sure your article answers the questions who, what, where, when, and why.

3. Create a classroom newspaper by collecting everyone's articles.

   EP017 Frontier America © Highsmith® Inc. 2007

Buffalo

The American Bison, or buffalo, was the source of many products for the Native Americans. Not only was the buffalo a good source of meat, but the hides were also used as clothes, shoes, tents, and more. No part of the buffalo went unused, and the buffalo could provide almost everything that a tribe needed.

When settlers began moving west, they also began hunting buffalo. However, the settlers were more careless about their use of the buffalo, and would even hunt just for sport. When the transcontinental railroad was built, the buffalo lost their land, and were often killed to clear them from the area around the tracks. In 1889, there were less than 1,000 buffalo alive in the wild and they were named an endangered species.

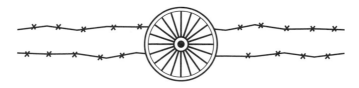

Project
Create a buffalo hide painting.

Materials
- paper bags
- crayons

Directions
1. Cut a paper bag open and lay flat. Tear off the edges so they are rough.
2. Create a hunting scene on the paper bag. Look at pictures of Native American art to get ideas on how to depict your hunting scene.
3. Crumple the bag, then flatten to create a rough hide look.

Blacksmith

Frontier townspeople depended a great deal on the work of the blacksmith. His job was to make and repair iron objects. He served homemakers as well as the trade workers in town. The iron was heated to a red glow and then hammered into shape by hand.

One of the most important items made by the frontier blacksmith was the horseshoe, made to protect the feet of horses. Each blacksmith had a different set of skills, depending on the area where he lived. Blacksmiths could also fix wagon wheels and farm supplies, and make tools and nails.

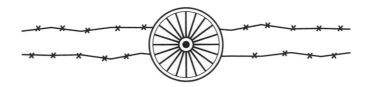

Project
Make a catalog for your own blacksmith shop.

Materials
- paper, folded in half
- pencil or pen

Directions
1. If you had a blacksmith shop, what would you name it, and where would it be? What would you make?

2. On the inside of the folded paper, show the items that you would make in your shop. Write what each item is used for, and who would be interested in buying each item. Put more items on the back if you choose.

3. Illustrate and color your catalog. Draw a picture and put the name of your blacksmith shop on the front.

Cowboys

A horse was a cowboy's most important possession. It was his only form of transportation and helped him earn a living. A cowboy had to be a good horseman, as he lived in the saddle for many hours every day. Rope was the cowboy's most important tool. He used it to catch cattle, hold his horse, pull wagons across muddy rivers, hold his packs in place, and kill snakes. Cowboys became adept with using a rope about 40 feet (12 m) in length, called a *lariat*.

Clothing was very simple and practical—boots, trousers, a wool shirt, jacket or vest, and a hat. Cowboys wore leather chaps to protect their legs from prickly sagebrush. Their hats had a wide brim to shield the cowboys' eyes against the hot sun and a deep crown to keep the hat from blowing off. They also used their hats as buckets! A bandanna could be pulled over the face as a filter against dust.

Cowboys on long cattle drives worked up huge appetites, and cooking from wagons was a difficult task. Colonel Charles Goodnight of Texas bought a war-surplus munitions wagon and constructed a "trail kitchen" on the back. That helped make work much easier for the cattle-drive cook. A large box was built in the back of an ordinary wagon. It had a hinged door that served as a work table when lowered. Inside there were storage shelves. The chuck wagon stocked pots, pans, tin cups, and eating utensils. The storage box was filled with sugar, coffee beans, bacon, lard, and sourdough starter for making hearty biscuits.

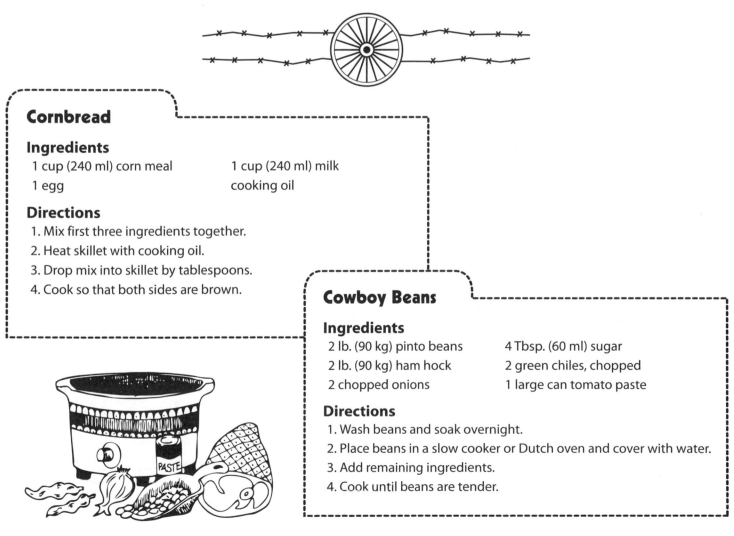

Cornbread

Ingredients
1 cup (240 ml) corn meal   1 cup (240 ml) milk
1 egg   cooking oil

Directions
1. Mix first three ingredients together.
2. Heat skillet with cooking oil.
3. Drop mix into skillet by tablespoons.
4. Cook so that both sides are brown.

Cowboy Beans

Ingredients
2 lb. (90 kg) pinto beans   4 Tbsp. (60 ml) sugar
2 lb. (90 kg) ham hock   2 green chiles, chopped
2 chopped onions   1 large can tomato paste

Directions
1. Wash beans and soak overnight.
2. Place beans in a slow cooker or Dutch oven and cover with water.
3. Add remaining ingredients.
4. Cook until beans are tender.

How the West Was Sung

Cowboys spent many long, boring hours on the trail. They often sang songs to pass time and to soothe the herd.

Most often the words to a song were set to an existing tune. The song was then passed to others to be added to and altered. There could be hundreds of verses. If a tune had more notes than the cowboy had words, he would sometimes hum or add nonsense words like "whoopee ti-yi-yo" until he could think of the next verse.

Learn and sing this cowboy song together.

As I was out walk-ing one morn-ing for pleas-ure, I spied a cow-punch-er a-rid-in' a-long. His hat was throwed back and his spurs were a jing-lin', And as he ap-proached he was sing-in' this song: Whoo-pee Ti - Yi - Yo Git A-long Lit-tle Do-gies, it's your mis-for-tune and none of my own, Whoo-pee Ti - Yi - Yo, Git A-long Lit-tle Do-gies, you know that Wy-o-ming will be your new home.

EP017 Frontier America © Highsmith® Inc. 2007

Frontier Homes

The homes on the frontier, from the Appalachians in the east to the Rockies in the west, were as varied as the settlers themselves. People needed shelter and the pioneers had to make do with what they found in the wilderness.

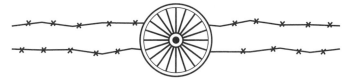

Project
Build models of frontier homes individually or in groups.

Materials:
- cardboard boxes
- brown paint and paintbrush
- twigs and grass
- scrap paper
- brown, green, white, and gray construction paper
- self-hardening clay
- plastic tub
- small pebbles or rocks

Lean-to
Settlers needed temporary shelter before winter weather arrived. They built a structure called a *lean-to*, or a half-camp. It was three-sided, facing away from the normal direction of the wind. The open side faced a fire that burned night and day. The back wall was often a pile of large, fallen logs. The remaining sides and roof were built from twisted bark and branches.

Directions
Build the model on a large cardboard box with one side cut out. Begin by painting the box with brown paint. Glue sticks and twigs to the remaining sides. Add detail—tall trees, a burning fire, animals, and so on.

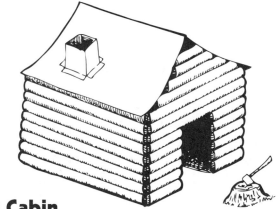

Log Cabin
When spring arrived, Appalachian pioneers were able to cut down trees, shape the wood into logs, and build log cabins. Neighbors helped each other with the job of lifting the heavy logs. The ends of the logs were notched to lock together. A chimney was built on one wall. Window openings were sometimes covered with animal skin or oiled paper, but usually were uncovered.

Directions
Roll paper logs from brown construction paper. Glue them on top of each other to form a four-sided house. Add a construction paper chimney. Leave openings for windows and a door. Add a roof with folded construction paper.

Frontier Homes

Soddy

The farmers on the great plains built dirt homes called soddies. Furrows of sod were plowed and cut into blocks 1-foot (.3-m) square. Blocks were piled in rows to make walls and covered with a thatched roof. The soddies were sometimes improved by hauling in lumber for doors and ceilings, and whitewashing the walls.

Directions

Shape self-hardening clay into 1-inch (2.54 cm) blocks. Stack to create the four walls, moistening the rows to hold them together. Paint with a thin, white tempera wash. Add a paper roof covered with dried grass.

Texas Ranch House

A ranch house consisted of two log cabins joined by an open, roofed space. One side was for sleeping, the other for cooking.

Directions

Cut doorways in two shoeboxes. Connect the boxes with cardboard. Cover with folded paper or craft sticks. Paint brown. Mount to cardboard, add details—corral, horses, cowboy bunkhouse, etc.

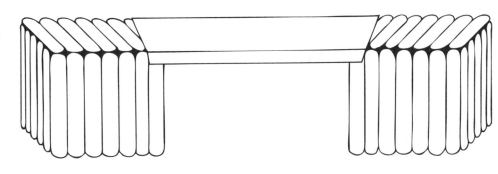

Miner's Rock House

A miner often slept outdoors in summer and built a crude shack in winter. He might have a tent or make a shelter out of rocks, empty boxes, or packing cases lined with newspaper for warmth.

Directions

Cut an opening in a plastic tub. Cover with small rocks or pebbles—aquarium rock will work—held by rubber contact cement. Line the inside with newspaper scraps. Mount on cardboard. Surround with details—pick and ax, mining pan, gold nuggets, burro, claim stake, etc.

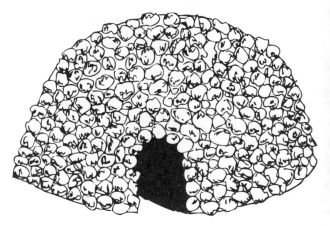

EP017 Frontier America © Highsmith® Inc. 2007

Farming Methods and Machines

After moving to the west and settling on their land, the pioneers found it more difficult to farm. The soil of the prairies was thicker and grew more grass than the sandy soil of New England. The cast-iron plows that they had used in the past didn't work on this prairie soil. In 1837, a plow was invented that had a steel blade. This steel blade was better able to slice through the soil, and the soil didn't stick to the blade. This plow was hitched to horses or oxen and pulled while the farmer walked behind it and guided the animal. Even with this new invention, plowing was not easy, but the steel plow helped to make the farmer's job less back-breaking.

The windmill was another invention that made farm life easier. One of the most important uses for the windmill was to pump water. Water for families and animals usually had to be pumped from the ground, and the windmill made this task easier.

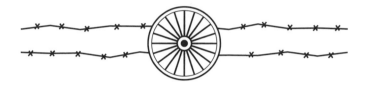

Project
Make a then and now chart about farm tools.

Materials
- research materials
- notebook paper
- pencil or pen

Directions
1. Research farm tools from the frontier era and the tools and machines used today.

2. On a piece of paper draw three columns. Label one "Task," the second "Then," and the third "Now." Leave enough room for both text and a picture for each tool.

3. Write the tools you researched in the appropriate columns, making sure to keep similar tools next to each other. Draw pictures of each tool.

4. Have a class discussion about your findings. How are tools different today? How are they similar?

Salt Sampling

Salt was extremely valuable to the pioneers. It was used for seasoning food and preserving meat. Although salt was used extensively, it was very difficult to obtain.

Native Americans showed the settlers where to locate *salt licks* (exposed natural salt on the ground). Once each year, some settlers would band together and journey to the salt licks. While there, the settlers would do some hunting because so many animals came to lick the salt.

The men would then gather enough salt to last the whole settlement for an entire year.

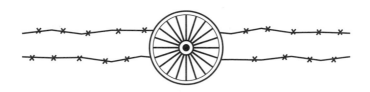

For the Teacher

Project

Make salt in your classroom.

If you live near a salt water supply, bring several buckets to class. If you do not live near a body of salt water, simply use tap water and add a box of salt. The results should be the same.

Materials

- large kettle
- hot plate
- box of salt (if not using salt water)

Directions

1. Measure the water as you fill a large kettle. Place the kettle on a hot plate. Add a measured box of salt to the water, if needed.

2. During the course of the day, observe the changing water level. Discuss evaporation and add more water. Keep track of the quantity added. Students can take turns adding water, with adult supervision.

3. When all the water has been evaporated (or the school day is over), measure the salt. Let each student sample a bit.

EP017 Frontier America © Highsmith® Inc. 2007

Brand-Name Ranchers

Cattle ranching was a major business on the frontier. Ranchers found they had to protect their cattle from being lost or stolen. Each rancher created a design called a brand from a combination of letters and symbols. With a branding iron, the brand was registered with county or state authorities. The brand was burned into the cattle's hide as a form of identification.

Many ranches were also named after the brand. Some examples are:

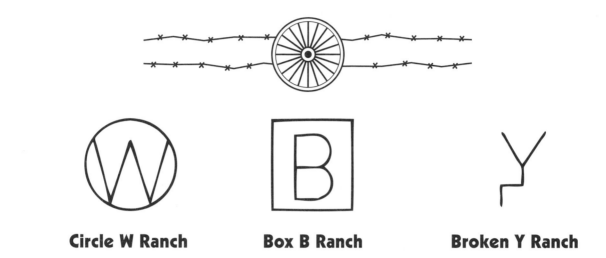

Circle W Ranch   **Box B Ranch**   **Broken Y Ranch**

Project

Pretend you own a cattle ranch on the frontier. Design a brand that will name your ranch and identify your cattle. You can use your initials or a combination of the symbols on the Branding Iron Chart. You can change any of the symbols to suit your ideas. For example, Crazy R can become Crazy M if your name begins with the letter "M."

Materials

- paper
- black or brown crayon
- butcher paper or brown grocery bag
- sponge or potato

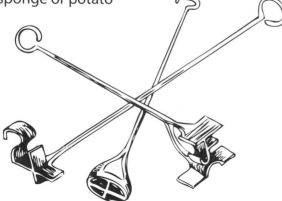

Directions

1. Make a rough sketch of your brand using black or brown crayon.
2. Then make a final drawing on a crumpled paper bag or use cut sponge or potatoes to make prints.
3. Register your brand. Reproduce the design on an index card and file it with the county "registrar." (This can be an elected or appointed position.)

Branding Iron Chart

Rocking 7	Running W	Crazy R	Lazy R
Flying 7	Hooked Y	Forked Y	Triple K
Bar	Double Bar	Broken Bar	Slash
Half Circle	Circle	Double Circle	Half Box
Double Box	Triangle	Diamond	Open A
Rocking Chair	Broken Heart	Spur	Stirrup
Sunrise	Broken L	Tumbling R	Reverse R

EP017 Frontier America © Highsmith® Inc. 2007

Frontier Transportation

In the very beginning, wagons and horses were the common forms of transportation on the frontier. As the population increased, a form of public transportation was needed, so most people began traveling by stagecoach. A group could defend more easily than a lone rider against attacking Native Americans or bandits. Stagecoaches often carried strong boxes filled with precious cargo that made them prey to robbery.

The coaches covered 100 miles (161 km) in 24 hours. Passengers, facing dust in the summer and cold in the winter, tried to sleep on hard seats as they bumped along. Swing stations were staggered every 10 to 15 miles (16 to 24 km) along the road, providing travelers a chance to rest and stretch.

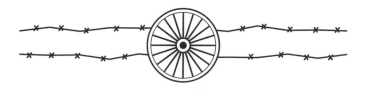

For the Teacher

Project

The stagecoach driver is driving the class somewhere ... but where? Play stagecoach 20 Questions to find out.

Directions

1. Before class, make slips of paper with frontier America places and landmarks, such as Independence, MO, Independence Rock, California Trail, Chimney Rock, etc.

2. Choose a stagecoach driver to begin.

3. Stagecoach driver picks a slip of paper—this is the destination of the stagecoach.

4. The class may raise their hands and ask questions one at a time. Keep track of the number of questions asked, limit the class to 20 questions.

5. The student who guesses the destination gets to be the next stagecoach driver!

Boom Town

Frontier towns seemed to be built overnight as centers for cattle transporting, mining, and shipping. These instant towns were called *boom towns*. There were few comforts in these boom towns. Tents provided shelter for most of the people. However, many homes were built from rocks, bottles, or packing cases. The towns were dusty and often filled with more cattle than people.

Main Street buildings were built in a hurry, too. Some businesses just pitched a tent. Others were simple frame structures with impressive false fronts.

The first boom town was built in 1867 in Abilene, Kansas. The last boom town was the busiest—Dodge City, Kansas. There were, however, many more towns scattered across the West.

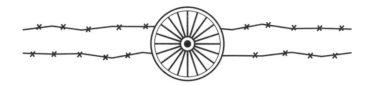

Project
Contribute to the construction of Main Street in a western boom town.

Materials
- tagboard
- construction paper
- shoebox
- cereal box

Directions
1. Cut a simple store front from tagboard, construction paper, or a cereal box. Glue the store front shape to the end of a shoebox. Add detail—windows, door, sign.

   Some of the buildings found in a boom town were:

Saloon	Hotel
Town Hall	Telegraph Office
Barber	Boarding House
General Store	Asseyor's Office
Blacksmith	

For the Teacher
Assemble all the buildings and place them side by side. Students may want to add more to the town—stick sidewalks, raffia tumbleweeds, hitching posts, etc. They can also create dioramas depicting the businesses.

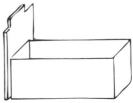

EP017 Frontier America © Highsmith® Inc. 2007

The Pony Express

The Pony Express was a service that transported mail by means of daring riders on horseback. The route began in St. Joseph, Missouri and traveled along the Oregon–California Trail. The riders braved rough trails, harsh weather, and Native American attacks. Their route took them along the Platte River in Nebraska, north of the Great Salt Lake, and across the Sierra Nevada Mountains to the final destination of Sacramento, California.

Pony Express riders rode at top speed from one station to the nest—about 75 miles (120 km). Every 10–15 miles (16–24 km), a fresh horse was supplied. As the rider approached the station a keeper brought out a fresh horse, and a new rider took over for the next 75–100 miles (120–160 km).

There were 80 riders in all, each earning $100–$150 a month. Mail was carried in leather, rainproof pouches strapped to the front of the saddle.

In the beginning, the postage rate was $5 per half ounce (14 g). By the end, the postage rate had dropped to $1 per half ounce. The mail usually took eight or nine days to reach its final destination. However, depending on the weather and the season, it could take up to two weeks.

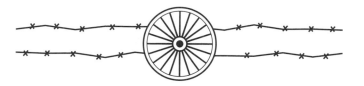

Projects

Station-to-station Relay: Divide into teams. Spread out at equal distances across the field. The first person has an envelope in his or her hands.

At the starting signal, the first team member begins running. When he or she reaches the second member of the team, the envelope is passed just like in a baton relay. The team of "riders" that passes the mail the fastest is the winner.

Postage Rates: Find out how much it costs to send a half ounce of mail at current rates. How does this compare to the Pony Express?

Calculate how much it would cost to send letters and packages by way of the Pony Express. Weigh several items on a scale. If they cost a $1 per half ounce, how much do they cost? Make a chart of the costs.

1860
1861

Pony Express Trail

Tell a Tale

Storytelling was a popular leisure-time activity. As stories were passed along from trail to trail and home to home, they became greatly exaggerated. Some were humorous, while others told of courageous acts and daredevil deeds. Western adventurers, explorers, peace officers, and outlaws alike became legendary due to this simple frontier recreation.

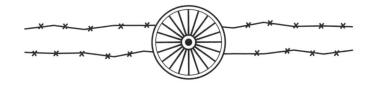

Projects

Select a name from one of the lists and find out more. Do one of the following:

- Write a short report.
- Dress up as this person and tell your story to the class.
- Make a poster collage depicting three to five events in this person's life.

Use your imagination and make up your own frontier legend.

- Create a name.
- Tell why he or she is best remembered.
- Describe an amazing accomplishment.
- Write a physical description.

Western Frontier Life

The Pioneers
Judge Roy Bean
Billy the Kid
Buffalo Bill Cody
Calamity Jane
Wyatt Earp
Bat Masterson
Annie Oakley
Belle Starr

Other Western Legends

Sitting Bull
Geronimo
Paul Bunyan
Johnny Appleseed
Pecos Bill
Nat Love
Sequoyah

Leaders of the Westward Movement

Daniel Boone
Kit Carson
William Clark
Meriwether Lewis
Davy Crockett
Samuel Houston
Zebulon Montgomery Pike
Brigham Young
Sacajawea

Frontier Recreation

Almost any event on the frontier was turned into a contest. Men, women, and children participated in apple paring, logrolling, cornhusking, and wood chopping, as well as spelling bees. Men often competed in shooting matches.

Once or twice a year, cowboys from several ranches in the area rounded up the cattle on the open range and herded them to a central location. Here they sorted the cattle according to their brands and branded any new calves. This roundup was both a time for work and for social events. As many as 300 cowboys participated in an athletic contest called a *rodeo* after their work was finished.

The men competed in bareback riding, steer wrestling, calf roping, and other tests of skill. They also gathered to share stories, sing songs, and make music. It is believed that the first rodeo ever held in the United States for spectators other than the participating cowboys was in Pecos, Texas, in 1883.

Children had their own games and toys, including homemade sleds and small wagons. They also had fun chasing hoops, skipping rope, and playing tag and other games. There was always plenty of food, fiddle-playing, and dancing for everyone, too!

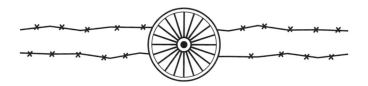

For the Teacher

Target Practice

Project
Here is a target-practice variation.

Materials
- beanbags
- stone
- chalk
- butcher paper
- paint

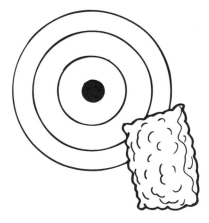

Directions
1. Make a target on a large square of butcher paper. Paint four circular bands in different colors. Paint the center circle red. This is the bull's eye.
2. Students can use a beanbag, or toss a stone marked with chalk. That way, when the stone strikes the target it can be easily marked.

Spelling Bee

Project
Hold a frontier spelling bee

Materials
- glossary

Directions
Use words from the glossary or make a list of the previous weeks' spelling words and hold a classroom spelling bee.

Indian War and American Indian Boarding Schools

From the time the first pioneers started moving west, there were always battles with the Native Americans over land. The Indian Removal Act was passed in 1830, which gave the government the right to move the Native American Tribes to reservation land. From 1838 to 1839, thousands of Cherokees were made to move. The Cherokee people were forced to walk for 116 days from northern Georgia to Oklahoma, a distance of about 1,200 miles (1,930 km). Around 4,000 died on this journey that is now known as the Trail of Tears.

In the late 1800s, new ideas of *assimilation* were put into practice. Assimilation is the absorption of a culture different than one's own. Americans viewed themselves as "cultured" and the Native Americans as "savages." Therefore, they started schools that taught Native American children how to behave and live "properly." In these schools, students' hair was cut, they were taught to live in the culture of white Americans, and they were forbidden to speak their native languages. Students were to give up their religion and take up Christianity.

A ritual known as the Ghost Dance was believed to bring ancestors back from the dead, restore animal life, and return native lands. This dance upset some of the settlers. They were scared that the Native Americans would revolt and take back their land. On December 29, 1890, the U.S. army rode into a Sioux camp at Wounded Knee Creek. A shot was fired, and by the time the army left, between 150 and 370 Sioux men, women, and children were dead, along with 31 soldiers.

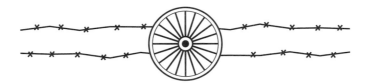

Project

Create a diary entry as a Native American student.

Materials

- notebook paper
- pen or pencil

Directions

1. Imagine that you are a Native American student who has been relocated to a different school. You have been forced to leave your family and adopt a new way of life. You must cut your hair, wear different clothes, learn a new language, and live by a new society's set of rules.

2. Write a diary entry. Describe what you are learning, how different it is, and how you feel about the situation.

EP017 Frontier America © Highsmith® Inc. 2007

California Gold Rush 1848–1849

In January of 1848, gold was discovered in California by a man named James Marshall. The news of this discovery spread quickly, and by the summer, people from all over the west were making their way to California in hopes of finding gold. By 1849, people from the eastern states were selling their possessions and traveling west, and some people even came from China! As time went on, the chances of successfully finding gold became much smaller because of the numbers of people looking for gold.

Miners often used a method called *panning*. This meant that a miner would put dirt in a pan and hold it under flowing water. The water would carry away the dirt and leave the heavier gold behind. By the end of 1849, most of the miners were unsuccessful because of the larger mining companies. These companies had more advanced technology to find gold. The hydraulic mining machines made it easier to find gold because more material could be processed faster than panning.

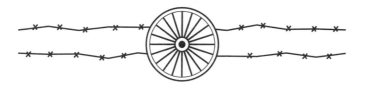

Project
Pan for gold!

Materials
- shovel
- sand and gravel
- sandpit or large tub
- water
- fool's gold or larger rocks painted gold
- gold pan or old dishpan
- tweezers
- dish to hold "gold"

Directions
1. Use a shovel to fill your gold pan half full with the sand and gravel mixture.
2. Fill your pan up with water.
3. Shake the pan in a circular motion. Tilt the edge farthest from you and let some of the gravel spill out of the pan. Lighter materials should be carried out of the pan along with some water.
4. Repeat until there is only a small amount of larger material left in the pan.
5. Add more water, and then gently swirl the pan. Because gold is more dense than sand, it should stay in the center while the lighter material moves to the outside.
6. Look for gold nuggets. Pick out the gold with tweezers and place it in your bowl. When you feel you have found all the gold, discuss with your classmates whether or not you thought panning for gold was easy. Can you think of a better method for finding gold?

For the Teacher
Fill the large tub with the sand and gravel mixture, sprinkling "gold nuggets" throughout.

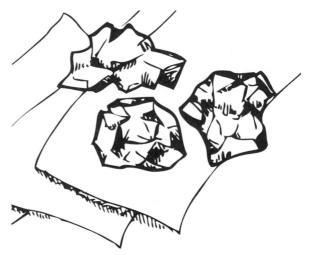

"Buffalo" Bill Cody

Buffalo Bill Cody is one of the American west's most popular and well-known figures. It is not known whether most of the stories about Buffalo Bill's life are true, but they are very popular tales. Buffalo Bill served in the Pony Express, was a scout in the Civil War, and worked for the Kansas Pacific Railroad. One of the stories of Buffalo Bill's adventures tells that he killed over 4,000 buffalo in 18 months, which is why he is called "Buffalo" Bill. In 1883, Buffalo Bill started his "Wild West Show" which romanticized life in the American west. In the Wild West Show, mock battles were held between Native Americans and Cowboys and the performers showed off their shooting skills.

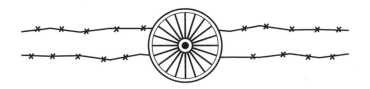

Project
Compare and contrast Buffalo Bill's view of the American west to the real thing.

Directions
1. As a class, brainstorm images that come to mind when you think of the old west. These should come from popular culture.
2. Think about what you have learned about the real frontier America. How are these images different from and similar to the images portrayed in popular culture?
3. Make a T-chart detailing things you know about frontier America. Write whether they are Fact or Myth.

For the Teacher
As students are brainstorming, help them come up with ideas from popular culture—toys, games, movies, etc. Make a classroom chart.

FRONTIER AMERICA

Fact   **or**   **Myth?**

EP017 Frontier America © Highsmith® Inc. 2007

Literature List

There are many fine books on aspects of frontier and pioneer life. Your librarian can recommend additional titles.

Bill Pickett: Rodeo Ridin' Cowboy
by Andrea Davis Pinkney. Gulliver Books, 1996. 32 p. Gr. 2–4
Describes the life and accomplishments of the son of a former slave whose unusual bulldogging style made him a rodeo star.

Bronco Charlie and the Pony Express
by Marlene Targ Brill. Carolrhoda Books, 2004. 46 p. Gr. 2–4
Tells the story of 11-year-old Charlie Miller, who became the youngest rider for the Pony Express.

Cowboys and Longhorns
by Jerry Stanley. Crown, 2003. 88 p. Gr. 5–6
A look at the fascinating and true story of how Texas Longhorns were run from Texas to Kansas so they could be shipped to meet the new demand for beef in the eastern U.S.

Lewis and Papa: Adventure on the Santa Fe Trail
by Barbara Joosse. Chronicle, 1998. 40 p. Gr. 2–4
While accompanying his father on the wagon train along the Santa Fe Trail, Lewis discovers what it is to be a man.

More Perfect Than the Moon
by Patricia MacLachlan. Joanna Cotler, 2004. 96 p. Gr. 3–5
Eight-year-old Cassie Witting is upset when she finds out that her mother, Sarah, is expecting a baby, but writing in a journal helps her sort out her feelings. The fourth in the series of stories set on the prairie in the nineteenth century that began with *Sarah, Plain and Tall*.

My America: Westward to Home: Joshua's Oregon Trail Diary
by Patricia Hermes. Scholastic, 2002. 112 p. Gr. 3–6
In 1848, nine-year-old Joshua Martin McCullough writes a journal of his family's journey from Missouri to Oregon in a covered wagon. Includes a historical note about westward migration. First in a series.

A Packet of Seeds
by Deborah Hopkinson. Greenwillow Books, 2004. 32 p. Gr. K–4
When a pioneer family moves west, the mother misses home so much that she will not even name the new baby until her daughter thinks of just the right thing to cheer her up.

Pecos Bill
by Bill Balcziak. Compass Point Books, 2003. 32 p. Gr. 2–4
This is a tall tale about the baby Pecos Bill being raised by coyotes and his eventual marriage to Slue-Foot Sue, another legend from the American southwest.

A Pioneer Sampler: The Daily Life of a Pioneer Family in 1840
by Barbara Greenwood. Houghton Mifflin, 1998. 240 p. Gr. 3–6
Chronicles one year in the lives of the imaginary Robinson family on the frontier.

The Toughest Cowboy: Or How the Wild West Was Tamed
by John Frank. Simon & Schuster, 2002. 48 p. Gr. K–3
How do you tame the roughest, toughest pack of cowboys to ever ride the open range?

Glossary

assimilation—the absorption of a culture different than one's own

bandanna—square piece of fabric that cowboys tied around the neck to absorb perspiration and to protect against breathing dust on the trail

barbed wire—double-stranded wire with barbs attached to keep cattle corralled and out of farmers' homesteads

boom town—a town that was "built overnight"

branding iron—iron tool used to "brand" a rancher's cattle for identification

buckskin—skin of a male deer, often made into clothing or shoes

cactus—succulent spiny plants native to desert regions; plural: cacti

calf—young or newborn cattle

chaps—leather leggings worn by cowboys to protect against pricks from sagebrush and from snake bites

cholera—an infectious bacterial disease

Conestoga wagon—large covered wagon used by pioneers

Cumberland Gap—the first trail west through the Appalachian Mountains

dogie—a motherless calf in a cattle herd

flapjacks—pancakes

flatboat—flat-bottomed boat used to transport people and supplies down a river

ford—cross a stream at a shallow place

Ghost Dance—a ritual believed to bring ancestors back from the dead

gingham—cotton cloth with a checked pattern

lariat—rope used to lasso cattle

lean-to—a temporary shelter, also called a half-camp

Manifest Destiny—the idea that America had the right to control all of the land between the Atlantic and Pacific

Morse code—a code in which the letters of the alphabet are represented by signals of sound or light

outlaw—a person who has broken the law

panning—a method miners used to find gold

parchment—stiff material used to write on, made from animal skins

perpetuity—something that lasts forever

prairie schooner—smaller covered wagon used by pioneers to travel across the country

ristra—the Spanish word for "string"; a long string of chili peppers

rodeo—competitions to test the skills of cowboys; they were held by the cowboys during roundups and cattle drives

roundup—bringing cattle together to count the herd and brand the new calves

salt licks—deposits of natural salt exposed on the ground

savage—a primitive, uncivilized person

scout—person hired to go ahead of the wagon train to look for danger, hostile Native Americans, or other problems on the trail

scow—a large, flat boat

sinew—a ligament or tendon

soddy—a dirt home

telegraph—a way to send messages across a wire

treacherous—dangerous or hazardous

wagon master—person of authority chosen by the families preparing to travel west

wagon train—a line of several wagons traveling across the country

EP017 Frontier America © Highsmith® Inc. 2007

Look what doesn't come from Japan!

Ninja is a Japanese word that refers to a kind of real-life warrior who lived hundreds of years ago. The **Teenage Mutant Ninja Turtles,** however, are not a Japanese creation. They were invented by American cartoonists Kevin Eastman and Peter Laird in 1983, and later became famous on television and in movies.

Meet the Author

Miles Harvey is the author of several books for young people. He lives in Chicago with his wife, Rengin, and daughter, Azize.

Look What Came From

Japan

by
Miles Harvey

Franklin Watts

A Division of Grolier Publishing

New York London Hong Kong Sydney

Danbury, Connecticut

Series Concept: Shari Joffe
Design: Steve Marton

Library of Congress Cataloging-in-Publication Data

Harvey, Miles.

                 / by Miles Harvey.
   p. cm. — (Look what came from)
  Includes bibliographical references and index.
  Summary: Describes many things that originated in
Japan, including inventions, art, food, fashion, furniture,
toys, animals, musical instruments, and sports.
   ISBN 0-531-11500-3 (lib.bdg.)   0-531-15966-3 (pbk.)
   1. East and West—Juvenile literature.   2. Japan—
Civilization— Juvenile literature.   [1. Japan—Civilization.]
I. Title. II. Series.
CB251.H28   1999
952—dc21   98-35845
                                  CIP
                                    AC

Visit Franklin Watts on the Internet at:
http://publishing.grolier.com

Photo credits © : Animals Animals: 18 left (Gerard Lacz); ENP Images: 19 left (Gerald Allen); Envision: front cover top left, 12 left, 8 right (Simon Feldman), 12 right, 14 right (Steven Needham), 18 right (Gary Crandall), 19 right (J. B. Marshall), 22 right (Hidemitsu Kaito); Cameramann International, Ltd.: 10 left, 22 left, 25 bottom right, 27 top right; Charise Mericle: 5; Christie's Images: 6 left, 6 right, 24; Dave Bartruff: 13, 17 top; Fujifotos: front cover top right, 7 right, 15 left, 17 bottom; Kyodo News: front cover bottom right, 11 right, 21 left; Monkmeyer Press Photo Service: 25 top right (Mimi Forsyth); NHPA: 21 top right (Kevin Schafer); Patricia Rasch: origami illustrations on 26-27; Photofest: 32 left; Photo Researchers, Inc.: 8 left (Blair Seitz), 21 bottom right (Tom McHugh), 25 top left (Renee Lynn), 25 bottom left (Yann Guichaoua); Photri: stamp on back cover, border on pages 4 and 6-32, 4 bottom left (Will & Deni McIntyre), 15 right; Rengin Altay: 32 right; Sony Electronics: 9 left; Superstock: front cover background, 4 bottom center, bottom right, 11 left, 14 left, 16 left, 17 middle, 1, 23 (Private Collection/Diana Ong); 3, 16 middle (David David Gallery, Philadelphia), Tony Stone Images: 9 right (Mel Lindstrom), 16 right (Paul Chesley), 20 (Art Wolfe)

Contents

Greetings from Japan!

Japan is a country made up of thousands of little islands. These islands are located in the Pacific Ocean. They are considered part of the continent of Asia. Japan is not a big country, but it is a very important one. Japanese people came up with the ideas for many things in your everyday life—from the video games you play to some of foods you eat. So, come on! Let's look at all the amazing things that come from Japan!

Japanese paper money

Japanese coins

The flag of Japan

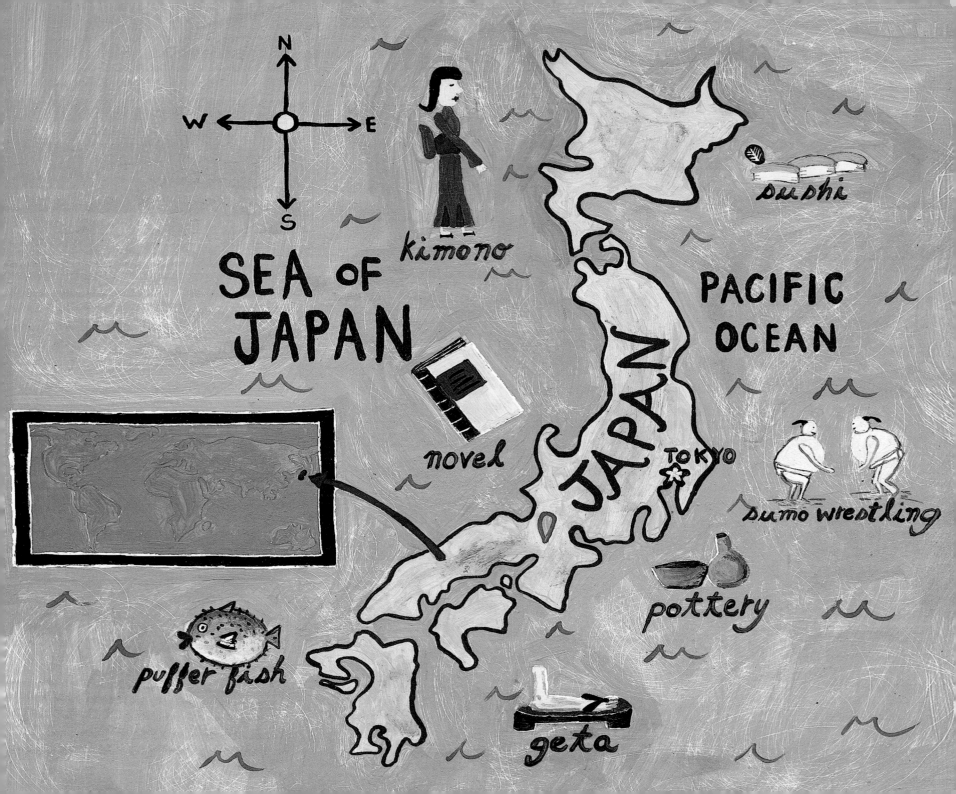

Inventions

Nobody knows exactly who came up with the idea of using clay to make pots, bowls, plates, and cups. But the oldest **pottery** in the world comes from the island of Honshu, which is part of Japan. People on this island were making pottery 13,000 years ago!

Ancient Japanese pottery

A **novel** is a wonderful kind of book. It is not about things that actually happened. Instead, it is a story that comes from the author's imagination. Many experts think

An ancient painting showing scenes from *The Tale of Genji*

Have you ever slept on a **futon?** A futon is special type of mattress that does not have springs inside. Instead, it is stuffed with cotton. The Japanese have been sleeping on futons for hundreds of years.

Today, lots of people in other countries love to relax on this comfortable kind of furniture.

the first novel was written by a Japanese woman named Murasaki Shikibu nearly 1,000 years ago. It was called *The Tale of Genji.*

Futon

7

People using a VHS videocassette recorder

Walkman

more

Many modern inventions also came from Japan. For example, a Japanese company invented the **VHS home video system** in 1975. This is the type of video equipment most people use today. It allows you to watch videotapes of movies and TV shows on your home television. The **Walkman personal stereo** was created in Japan in 1979. This little machine allows you to listen to your favorite music no matter where you are.

inventions

People from Japan also created the **digital video disk.** These disks are beginning to replace VHS videotapes. When you go to the video store in the future, you may get disks instead of tapes.

CD-ROM

Digital video-disk recorder

In 1984, a Japanese company came out with the first **CD-ROMs.** These disks allow you to play games and do lots of other cool stuff on your computer!

9

The Arts

Woman doing ikebana

Ikebana is the Japanese art of flower arrangement. Today, many people in other countries practice this art. The point of ikebana is not to use lots of flowers. Instead, the idea is to combine just the right flowers with just the right vase to make a beautiful and simple arrangement. It's not as easy as you might think!

Haiku is a kind of Japanese poetry. Like ikebana, haiku emphasizes simplicity. There are only a few words in each haiku poem. The idea is to pick the perfect words for every poem!

Haiku poems usually are made up of three lines. The first line has 5 syllables, the second has 7 syllables, and the third line has 5 syllables.

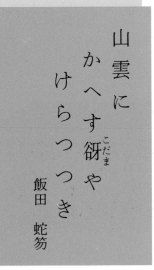

山雲に
かへす谺や
けらつつき
こだま

飯田 蛇笏

A haiku poem in Japanese

Yama-gumo ni
 kaesu kodama ya
  kera-tsutsuki

How the haiku would sound if read aloud

A woodpecker's drilling
Echoes
To the mountain clouds.
  -Iida Dakotsu

English translation of the haiku

Kabuki theater

Kabuki is a type of Japanese theater that involves singing, dancing, and beautiful makeup and costumes. Today, kabuki is often performed outside of Japan.

Kabuki actor

11

Food

The Japanese were probably the first people to grow mushrooms for food. People in Japan have been raising mushrooms for at least 2,000 years. Today, they still love to eat a yummy kind of mushroom called the **shiitake.**

Have you ever tasted **soy sauce?** Lots of people love to sprinkle this delicious liquid on their food. The Japanese came up with the idea for soy sauce more than 1,000 years ago.

Shiitake mushrooms

Many other great kinds of food also come from Japan. One tasty Japanese meal is called **sukiyaki.** It is made up of thin slices of meat, bean curd, and vegetables cooked in soy sauce and sugar. The word *sukiyaki* means "cooked

Soy sauce

12

on the blade of a plow." Japanese farmers used to cook sukiyaki over an outdoor fire, using their metal plow for a grill. People don't usually make sukiyaki that way anymore! Today you can get it at Japanese restaurants.

more food

Sushi rolled up
in seaweed

Have you ever tried eating raw fish? People in Japan do it all the time. They call this meal **sashimi.** The idea of eating uncooked fish might not sound very tasty. But you should go to a Japanese restaurant and give it a try. You might be in for a delicious surprise!

Shrimp and tuna
sushi

Another kind of food you can try at Japanese restaurants is **sushi.** Sushi is made by pressing cold cooked rice and vinegar into various shapes and adding raw or

Sashimi

Wasabi is a spicy paste made from this greenish Japanese root.

cooked fish or vegetables. Sometimes sushi is rolled up in seaweed. Sushi looks beautiful—and tastes even better!

People in Japan usually eat sashimi and sushi with soy sauce and a special kind of Japanese mustard called **wasabi.** Wasabi has a very strong and very spicy flavor!

Fashion

The **kimono** is a kind of robe that people in Japan have been wearing for hundreds of years. Today, the Japanese usually wear kimonos only on special occasions. But in other parts of the world, many people wear gowns or robes inspired by this beautiful type of clothing.

Geta are Japanese sandals made of wood. They are built a special way to keep your feet well above the dirt and mud!

Kimonos

Geta

Toys and Games

A family playing Super Mario Brothers

Japanese flower cards

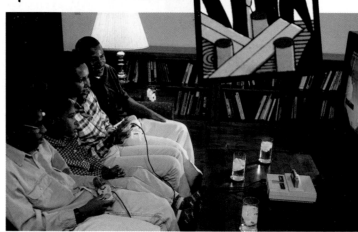

Lots of cool toys and games come from Japan. Some fun games use special kinds of playing cards called **Japanese flower cards.** In Japan, they are known as *hanafuda.* These cards are very colorful and pretty. They contain pictures of different kinds of plants and animals.

You may not have played any games that involve Japanese flower cards, but you've probably played other games from Japan. Many computer and video games, such as **Super Mario Brothers,** were invented in Japan.

Another fun toy from Japan is **Tamagotchi.** This is a tiny electronic pet that you can hold in the palm of your hand. By pressing buttons, you can feed it, play with it, and put it to bed.

Tamagotchi

Japanese bobtail

Animals

Akita

Japanese kids love to have cats as pets. One kind of cat from Japan has a very short tail. This type of cat is called a **Japanese bobtail.** Some Japanese bobtails are now raised elsewhere in the world.

Children in Japan also love dogs. One of their favorites is the **Akita.**

The **puffer fish** is an amazing animal. When a puffer fish is in danger, it blows itself

Fugu (left) and specially-trained chef preparing fugu (above)

up like a balloon so that other animals won't be able to fit it into their mouths. In Japan, this fish is called *fugu*. Some Japanese like to eat fugu because it is very delicious. However, it is also very poisonous. Only specially trained chefs can prepare fugu. They know how to remove the poisonous parts. If these parts aren't removed, a person who eats the fish can get very sick, or even die!

Japanese macaque

more animals

Monkeys are usually found in warm parts of the world. The **Japanese macaque,** however, is famous for being able to survive in very cold weather. Can you guess what its nickname is? The snow monkey!

Cormorants are big birds that love to dive underwater. For about 1,000 years, fishermen in Japan have been getting an unusual kind of help from these birds. The fishermen tie strings around the necks of the cormorants. When the birds swim underwater, they bring back fish for their human co-workers!

Another cool kind of Japanese bird is the **short-tailed albatross.** Once, these birds could be found in lots of places.

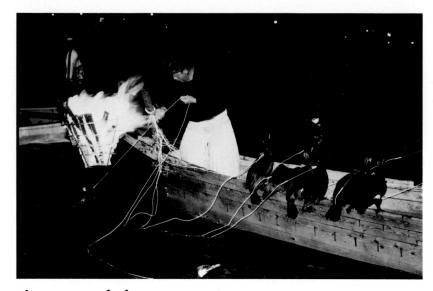

Japanese fisherman and cormorants

Short-tailed albatross

But because of hunting by human beings, only a few hundred short-tailed albatrosses remain. These days, short-tailed albatrosses make their nests at only one place on Earth— a little Japanese island in the Pacific Ocean.

Another interesting animal is the **Japanese giant salamander.** Most salamanders are only a few inches from head to tail. The Japanese giant salamander is almost 5 feet (1.5 m) long!

Japanese giant salamander

21

Musical Instruments

Taiko is an amazing kind of Japanese music played on drums. One of these drums is called the **o-daiko.** This drum sometimes weighs more than 660 pounds (297 kg). In fact, some o-daiko drums are so big that it takes two people to play them!

Koto

O-daiko drums

Another famous Japanese instrument is the **kokyu.** It has four strings and is played with a bow, sort of like a violin. Another instrument is the **koto.** It has 13 strings and is similar to a zither. The **samisen** has three strings and looks kind of like a guitar. One traditional kind of Japanese musical group consists of three women. One of them plays the kokyu, one of them plays the koto, and one of them plays the samisen.

Samisen

Kokyu

Sports

Do you know what martial arts are? They are sports similar to boxing and wrestling. The point of martial arts is to learn how to defend yourself. Many of the most famous martial arts come from Japan. One of them is **sumo wrestling.** This sport is 2,000 years old. It involves a wrestling match between two gigantic men.

In **aikido,** you learn how to turn back your opponent's attacks without attacking back. Aikido is designed to improve your body's flexibility, while giving you a stronger sense of discipline.

Another kind of Japanese martial art is **judo.** Like aikido, judo is supposed to improve your mind as well as your athletic skills. Judo was invented about 120 years ago. It is based on a much older Japanese martial art called **jujitsu.**

Another famous Japanese martial art is **kendo.** Students of this sport wear protective gear on their heads, chests, and hands. They battle against each other with springy swords made of bamboo.

Sumo wrestlers and referee

24

Aikido

Jujitsu demonstration

Judo

Kendo

A Craft from Japan

Learn an ancient art

In Japan, people make a beautiful kind of art without using any paint, crayons, or magic markers. They do it simply by folding pieces of paper! This type of art is called **origami.** No one knows exactly who first came up with the idea, but many people think it was invented in Japan nearly 1,500 years ago. Once you get very good at origami, you can make all kinds of animals. But for starters, let's try making a hat!

To start, you'll need a square piece of paper that is 22 inches wide and 22 inches long. You can use either wrapping paper or colored construction paper.

1. Put the paper flat on a table. The side that you want to be on the outside of the hat should be facing down. Take one of the corners of the paper and lift it toward you. Place it on the opposite corner. Then fold the paper in half. The paper should now look like a triangle.

2. Turn the triangle so that the folded part is facing you. Lift the right corner of the triangle. Then fold it over so that the point touches the opposite edge of the paper, halfway between the two other corners.

26

3. Lift up the left point. Fold it over the same way you did with the right point. The paper should now have five sides.

4. At the top corner, stick your fingers between the two halves of paper. Fold the half closest to you over as far as it will go.

5. Turn the paper completely over, so that the side that was against the table is now facing you. Then take the top corner of that side and fold it toward you as far as it will go. Take the opening at the top of the paper and pull the two sides away from each other a little bit.

6. Turn the whole thing over, and put the opening over the top of your head. Now you're wearing an origami hat!

How do you say....?

People in Japan speak Japanese. This language uses an alphabet that is very different from the one we use in English. If Japanese words look funny to you, imagine how strange English words look to kids from Japan!

English	Japanese	How to pronounce it
good morning	お早うございます	oh-high-yo guz-igh mus
good-bye	さようなら	suh-yun-oh-rah
dog	犬	inu
fish	魚	sa-ka-na
monkey	猿	sah-roo
mushroom	きのこ	kin-oh-koh
pottery	陶器	toh-gay
rabbit	兎	oo-sah-gee
soy sauce	醤油	shoh-yuh

To find out more

Here are some other resources to help you learn more about Japan:

Books

Haskins, Jim. **Count Your Way Through Japan.** Carolrhoda Books, 1987.

Kalman, Bobbie. **Japan: The Culture.** Crabtree Publishing, 1989.

Kalman, Bobbie. **Japan: The People.** Crabtree Publishing, 1989.

Littlefield, Holly. **Colors of Japan.** Carolrhoda Books, 1997.

McKay, Susan. **Festivals of the World: Japan.** Gareth Stevens, 1997.

Sato, Yoshio. **Animal Origami.** Kodansha, 1997.

Organizations and Online Sites

Japan Information and Culture Center
Embassy of Japan
1155 21st Street, NW
Washington, DC 20036-3308
http://www.embjapan.org/

Japan National Tourist Organization
One Rockefeller Plaza, Suite 1250
New York, NY 10111
http://www.jnto.go.jp/

Kid's Window—Japan
http://www.jwindow.net/KIDS/ kids_home.html
Discover cool stuff about Japanese arts and crafts, language, and food.

Kids Web Japan
http://www.jinjapan.org/kidsweb/
Learn about Japanese schools, sports, and politics on a site created especially for kids.

Map of Japan
http://www.lib.utexas.edu/Libs/ PCL/Map_collection/middle_east_ and_asia/Japan_rel96.jpg
Check out this online map of Japan, provided by the University of Texas at Austin.

Glossary

bean curd a soft, cheeselike food made from soybeans

CD-ROM a compact disc that you use in your computer

continent one of the major land areas of Earth

digital video disk a special kind of disk that plays video movies

discipline strict training that teaches self-control

flexibility the quality of being able to bend or twist easily

ninja a type of Japanese warrior

opponent someone who plays against you in a game or sport

plow a large tool used for breaking up or turning over the soil to prepare it for planting

poisonous dangerous if eaten or touched

simplicity the quality of being simple

zither a musical instrument having 30 to 40 strings stretched across a flat board; it is played by plucking the strings

Index